THE ORCHARD BOOK *of the*
LEGENDS OF
KING ARTHUR

D1512703

C152468470

KENT ARTS & LIBRARIES	
C152468470	

ORCHARD BOOKS

96 Leonard Street, London EC2A 4XD

Orchard Books Australia

32/45-51 Huntley Street, Alexandria, NSW 2015

ISBN 1 84362 593 8

First published in Great Britain in 1996

This edition published in 2004

Text © Andrew Matthews 1996

Illustrations © Peter Utton 1996

The right of Andrew Matthews to be identified as the author
and Peter Utton to be identified as the illustrator
of this work has been asserted by them in accordance
with the Copyright, Designs and Patents Act 1988.

A CIP catalogue record for this book is available from the British Library.

3 5 7 9 10 8 6 4 2

Printed in Singapore

THE ORCHARD BOOK *of the*
LEGENDS OF KING ARTHUR

RETOLD BY ANDREW MATTHEWS
ILLUSTRATED BY PETER UTTON

ORCHARD BOOKS

CONTENTS

CONTENTS

INTRODUCTION

ARTHUR IS THE MOST FAMOUS KING BRITAIN HAS ever had – much more famous than any of the kings in history books. No one knows if he was a real king or not, but stories about him are so well loved that people have tried to prove that he did exist.

If there was a real Arthur, he probably lived more than a thousand years ago. At that time Saxon and Danish people were invading Britain and Arthur may have been a leader who fought against them. No one really knows for sure, because over the years the story of Arthur has become a legend.

A legend starts off as a true story, but as the story is told over and over again, it gets mixed up with people's hopes and dreams. Some things are missed out, and new things are added along the way, and in the end facts and imagination run into one another so that it's impossible to tell which is which.

It's difficult to say exactly why Arthur was taken out of history and turned into a legend, and there are many different versions of his story. This is just one of them...

Chapter One
THE KING AND THE ENCHANTER

ONG, LONG AGO IN THE LAST DAYS OF magic, Britain was still a wild place. Eagles flew over the mountains. Bears and wild boar grunted and snuffled in the forests, and at night wolves howled at the moon. The last giant and dragon were long dead, but there were still enchanters, people who used the power of magic. The greatest of these was Merlin.

People began to tell stories about Merlin almost as soon as he was born. Some said he was from the south, others that he was from Wales, but where Merlin came from was as much a mystery as where he was going. Merlin came and went as he pleased and no one knew where or when he might appear. On one thing, however, everyone was agreed: Merlin was magic, and when he appeared strange things were certain to happen.

In those days Britain was ruled by King Uther. Uther was a strong man, but he was quick to do things without thinking first. Because of this, he made many mistakes and many enemies. Some of the dukes and earls of Britain secretly thought that they would make better rulers than Uther.

Then there came a dark time. Uther fell in love with the Lady Igraine, who was married to the Duke of Cornwall. And Uther made war against the duke in his castle at Tintagel. He killed the duke in battle, and the Lady Igraine and her young daughter were filled with grief and hatred. But the more Igraine hated Uther, the more he loved her, until he almost went mad because of it.

One night Uther was having dinner alone in the cold stone hall of his castle at Terrabil, when the flaming torches on the walls began to smoke. The smoke flowed into a corner, curled round on itself, grew darker and then turned into Merlin the Enchanter. The light of the torches threw moving shadows into Merlin's face. With his loose black robes and long hooked nose, the Enchanter looked like a huge dark bird.

"Wh-what do you want?" Uther asked.

"Your child," said Merlin.

Uther laughed out loud and took a drink from his wine cup to give himself courage. "You're mad! I haven't got a child!" he said.

"But you will have," Merlin told him. "A year after you marry the Lady Igraine, she will have your child."

Uther had drunk too much wine and it made his brain slow. "Marry Igraine?" he said. "But she hates me!"

"Listen!" said Merlin. "Love can be turned into hate and hate can be turned into love if you know how." He moved his fingers and the hall filled with the scent of roses.

"Could you make Igraine love me with magic?" Uther whispered.

"If you give me the child," said Merlin. He moved his fingers again and Uther seemed to see Igraine's face hanging in the air before him.

"Take the child!" exclaimed Uther. "Take anything you want – but make Igraine love me!"

The face vanished. Uther turned to say something to Merlin and found he was alone again.

Next morning, the king woke with a pounding head. The talk he remembered having with Merlin must have been a trick the wine had played on his mind, he thought. Yet in time, the Lady Igraine's hate did turn to love. She married Uther and he forgot all about Merlin.

But the death of the Duke of Cornwall was not forgotten. Many great lords met together in secret. They were afraid that if Uther could make war against the Duke of Cornwall, he would also make war against them. They decided to strike first.

Exactly a year after her marriage to King Uther, Igraine gave birth to a boy. He was born just before midnight. Uther was in another part of the castle getting ready for a battle at sunrise. When he heard the news he went clanking off to his wife's room in full armour.

He found Merlin waiting for him, cradling the baby in his arms. Igraine and her nurse were deep in a charmed sleep.

"Why have you come here?" asked Uther.

"To fetch the child you promised me," said Merlin.

"I was drunk when I made that promise!" said Uther. "I want my son to grow up here with me and Igraine!"

"If the boy stays here, he will die," said Merlin. "If your enemies knew you had a son, they would kill him at once to keep him from ever claiming the throne."

"No harm will come to my son while I live!" Uther said fiercely.

"I know," said Merlin. The way he said it made Uther's face turn white.

"Merlin," he said, "are you telling me that I'm going to be killed in the battle tomorrow?"

"Tomorrow's battle will start a civil war that will go on for years," Merlin said. "Brothers will kill one another and sons will fight their fathers. The only hope for peace is this child."

Uther didn't listen to Merlin. All he could hear was his frightened heart, pounding in his ears. "Can't you help me?" he asked. "Can't you cast a spell that will –"

"I came to take the child somewhere safe," said Merlin.

When the Enchanter carried the baby out of the room, Uther did nothing to stop him.

That same night, another baby was born. He was the son of Sir Ector, a knight who lived in a castle on the banks of the River Severn. Sir Ector already had a son, a six-year-old called Kay. Kay had been spoiled by his mother and Sir Ector had hoped that a younger brother would make him less greedy and selfish. The baby was to have been named Mark, but he died less than an hour after he was born, and his mother died not long after.

Sir Ector sat alone and let the tears stream down his face into his brown beard.

"At least I've got Kay," he whispered miserably.

"Kay needs a brother," said a voice.

"I know!" sniffed Sir Ector. "But what can I do? I –" He suddenly realised that someone was standing in the shadows in one corner of the room and his hand reached down for the dagger at his belt. "Who's there?" he called. "Come into the light where I can see you!"

Merlin the Enchanter stepped out of the darkness. He held out a bundle to Sir Ector – a bundle that wriggled and kicked.

"Merlin?" said Sir Ector. "What d'you want with me?"

"I want you to care for this child," Merlin said. "His name is Arthur. Raise him as if he were your own. He can be a brother to Kay and in time he'll be more than that – but be careful. Never tell anyone that I gave you the child – not even the boy himself."

Sir Ector felt confused. He wasn't sure what he should do, but just then the baby began to cry. The cry went straight to Sir Ector's heart and he reached out and took the small bundle from Merlin's hands.

Chapter Two
SWORD, ANVIL AND STONE

 AR RAGED FOR SIXTEEN YEARS. Villages were burned down. Men were too busy fighting to harvest and ungathered crops rotted in the fields. The air was thick with smoke and the wailing of new widows and orphans. The whole country was caught up in the fighting and the misery, hunger and disease that civil war brings with it.

At last, the great lords called a truce. They said that they were sick of war. Just before Christmas they met together in the hall of the cathedral at London to see if they could settle their arguments. First there was feasting and laughter, then there were curses and insults, and suddenly swords were drawn.

"Stop this!" thundered a voice.

The voice was loud enough for everyone to hear and cold enough to freeze them where they stood. Merlin walked through the hall, staring straight into the eyes of each man as he passed. No one could hold the Enchanter's gaze for long.

"While you squabble like dogs over a bone, Britain lies in ruins!" Merlin scolded. "It's time for peace!"

"There'll be no peace until we have a king!" said one of the lords. "Choose one of us, Merlin!"

Other voices called out in agreement, but Merlin shook his head. "High kings are born, not chosen," he said. "But I will make you a magic that will find him." Merlin circled his hands in the air and a light shone in through the windows of the hall. The light was so bright that the men covered their eyes .

"Follow me," said Merlin. "See what I have done."

It was cold outside the hall and the twilight air was grey. There in the churchyard stood a block of pure white marble. On top of the marble was an iron anvil and sunk deep into the anvil was a sword. The jewels on the hilt of the sword glowed softly in the last of the daylight. Written on the block in letters of gold were the words:

Whoever draws this sword from the anvil and the stone is the true-born High King of Britain.

"Go back to your castles," commanded Merlin. "Send messengers out to every knight in the land. Tell them that a tournament will be held in London on New Year's Day. The champions of the tournament will be the first to try and draw the sword."

The crowd of noblemen slowly left the churchyard until at last only one knight remained. It was Sir Gawain, a young man who was famous for his courage and his skills in battle. He gazed at the sword in the anvil and was deep in thought.

"What is it, Gawain?" Merlin asked. "Do you want to try and draw the sword?"

"Not me!" laughed Gawain. "I'm no true-born high king. But I'll fight on the side of the man who is, even if he turns out to be my worst enemy!"

"He won't be," Merlin said. "You and the high king will be close friends."

"You know who he is already, don't you?" said Gawain. Merlin said nothing, but he smiled. It was a thin, strange smile.

Chapter Three
THE SQUIRE

ARTHUR WAS A SQUIRE. THAT MEANT he could wear a short sword at his belt and dress in fine clothes on special occasions, but it also meant he was at the beck and call of his older brother, Kay. Kay was already a knight and should have known better, but he seemed to enjoy ordering Arthur about. He even made Arthur empty out his bathwater and groom his horse, treating him more like a servant than a squire and a brother.

Arthur could have complained to their father, but he knew that Sir Ector would only take Kay's part. Kay was the favourite and Sir Ector made no secret of it. Besides, Arthur wanted Kay to like him and he thought the best way to go about it was to do everything that Kay wanted without grumbling.

When he wasn't being Kay's skivvy, Arthur learned about being a knight. As a small boy, he had imagined that being taught how to hold a lance and use a sword would be exciting – but it wasn't. It was mostly doing the same things over and over again and still getting them wrong. His trainer, the master-at-arms, was stern but fair.

"You've got a lot to learn, but there's the makings of a knight in you, lad," he kept telling Arthur.

Arthur hated being called a lad. He was nearly as tall as Kay and felt quite grown up, but everyone treated him as though he was still a child.

The Christmas after Arthur's sixteenth birthday, a mysterious messenger arrived at the castle. Sir Ector saw him in private and then sent a servant to fetch Kay.

"Can't I go as well?" Arthur asked his brother.

"This is knights' business, not squires'," Kay replied haughtily. "Why don't you run along and play, like a good little boy?"

Arthur was dying to give Kay a kick for this insult, but he knew it would only cause trouble, so he went out into the courtyard to find a stone to kick instead. He noticed the messenger's servant guarding his master's horse. Arthur strolled over and pretended to admire the animal. Before long, he and the servant started to chat.

"There's going to be a big tournament in London," the servant said. "The biggest ever, so they say. My master's riding about inviting all the best knights to it."

"Really?" said Arthur.

"And that's not all," said the servant. "There's talk going around that at the end of the tournament the knights are going to choose a high king and put an end to the war. Of course, if you ask me..."

Arthur didn't listen to the rest. He wasn't interested in the business about the High King but the thought of going to a great tournament made his heart beat faster. He'd never been to London – he'd be able to wear the new clothes he'd been given for his birthday, and – a sudden thought made him panic. He rushed into the castle, almost colliding with the messenger who was coming down the staircase, and burst into Sir Ector's private chamber.

Sir Ector and Sir Kay stared at him in astonishment.

"You can't!" panted Arthur. "I mean – you mustn't! It wouldn't be fair!"

"What are you babbling about, boy?" snapped Kay.

"The tournament in London," said Arthur. "You are going to take me, aren't you?"

Kay's eyes went small with anger. "How dare you talk that way!" he hissed. "How dare you burst into my father's chamber! I can see you need a good ducking in the horse trough!"

"Leave the boy alone, Kay," said Sir Ector firmly. "He's got himself so excited that he's forgotten his manners. I know someone else who used to do that at his age."

Kay closed his mouth tight.

Sir Ector turned to Arthur with a warm smile. "Yes, you're coming to the tournament," he said. "You're to be Kay's shield-bearer."

"Thank you, Father!" gasped Arthur.

"I've told you before about calling me Father, boy," Sir Ector said. "You must always call me Sir Ector."

"Yes, Sir Ector," Arthur mumbled.

"Now go down to the stables and tell the grooms to make the horses ready," said Sir Ector. "We're leaving for London at daybreak tomorrow."

Chapter Four
SIR KAY THE FORGETFUL

 HE SNOW CAME IN FLURRIES AND THE cold wind rubbed Arthur's face raw, but he couldn't remember a time when he had been happier. In his young life he had never travelled so far before and it was like a dream.

Sir Ector, Kay and Arthur saw trim farmhouses. There were other knights and squires on the London road, and fine ladies riding inside silk-draped litters. They saw signs of war, too: burned-out villages whose ashes blackened the snow. Once, they had to move to the side of the road to let a band of lepers pass by.

They spent the first night in a monastery and Arthur fell asleep to the chanting of monks. The second night they stayed at an inn and Arthur hardly slept at all. He was kept awake by drunken voices singing songs with rude words.

On the morning of the third day they came to the outskirts of London and Arthur stopped his horse to gaze at the great city. In the distance he could see the tournament field which looked white because of all the tents pitched on it. Arthur felt excitement building up in his stomach and he urged his horse on.

A long way ahead, Sir Ector was talking to a knight he had met at the inn. Kay was dawdling behind, fiddling with his saddlebags and muttering under his breath. When Arthur drew level, Kay looked up, his face worried and pale.

"You haven't picked up my sword, have you?" he asked.

"No," said Arthur. "You told me that you'd set the hounds on me if I ever touched it, remember?"

Kay groaned and slapped himself on the forehead. "I've left it at the inn!" he groaned. "How could I be such an idiot? If I don't go back for it, I'll have no sword to use at the tournament and if I do go back, someone's bound to notice and ask me why. I'll be called Sir Kay the Forgetful for the rest of my days."

"Nobody would notice if I slipped away," said Arthur.

"You?" said Kay.

"I'll be back with the sword before anybody knows I've gone," Arthur vowed.

"All right," said Kay, "but, er, look, Arthur, you won't tell anyone else about this, will you?"

"I'm your brother," said Arthur. "I don't say bad things about you behind your back – well, not to other people, anyway."

Arthur felt happy as he galloped along the frosty road. Kay would be grateful to him when he brought the sword back. Perhaps he would be kind and behave more like a brother.

But when he reached the inn, Arthur's high hopes turned into dismay. The place was shut, the windows were boarded, the doors were barred and the only person in sight was an old man.

"Where's the innkeeper?" Arthur cried.

"Gone," replied the old man, "and taken 'is wife and 'is servants with 'im. They've all gone to the tournament, see. And where'm I goin' to get my mug of ale now, I'd like to know!"

"I didn't see them on the way," said Arthur. "What road have they taken?"

"That un," said the old man, pointing with his stick. "Past the cathedral churchyard, left at Gallows Field, right at the old kiln and then –"

Arthur didn't wait to hear any more. He turned his horse's head and kicked his heels into its sides.

It was hopeless. By the time he reached the churchyard, Arthur had forgotten what turning he was supposed to take next. If he carried on, he would only get lost.

He reined in his horse and came to a halt. There was no hope of Kay being kind now. Arthur had told his brother he would fetch his sword and he had let him down. The other young knights would make fun of Kay, and Kay would take it out on Arthur. And then, in the middle of all his dark thoughts, Arthur saw a sword.

Chapter Five

THE HIGH KING

IT WAS THE STRANGEST OF ALL THE strange things Arthur had seen on the journey, but he hardly paid it any attention. In the centre of the churchyard stood a block of marble, white and glistening. There were golden letters carved in the marble, but Arthur didn't notice them. On top of the marble block was an iron anvil, but Arthur didn't really notice that either. All he could see was the sword. Its richly jewelled hilt glittered above the top of the anvil; its blade ran straight down through the iron into the marble beneath.

Arthur hadn't stopped before barging into Sir Ector's private chamber, and he didn't stop to think now. Kay needed a sword and there was a sword. The anvil and the marble block didn't matter a whistle.

Arthur scrambled out of his saddle, clambered over the churchyard wall and wove his way between the tombstones. When he reached the white marble block, he stretched out his right arm and closed his fingers on the sword's hilt. He could see no join between the steel of the blade and the iron of the anvil, and for a moment he thought he might not be able to lift it, but when he pulled, the sword ran out smoothly and rang like a chiming bell. Arthur bounded back to his horse, waving the sword over his head and whooping with delight.

Kay was waiting where Arthur had left him. When he saw the sword in Arthur's hand he grinned and Arthur thought the grin was worth all his worry and effort.

"Well done!" said Kay, taking the sword. "If we hurry, I can –"

He left the sentence unfinished. He was staring at the sword and there was an expression on his face that Arthur didn't recognise.

"This isn't my sword, Arthur!" Kay whispered. "Where did you get it?"

"The cathedral churchyard," said Arthur. "The inn was shut, so I asked this old man which way –"

"The messenger told us the sword had a jewelled hilt," said Kay, and though he spoke out loud he was really talking to himself, "and its blade had been driven deep into an anvil standing on a block of white marble ..."

"How did you know?" laughed Arthur.

Kay didn't answer. He rode off at full speed, shouting Sir Ector's name at the top of his voice. Arthur tried to follow, but his horse was tired and he soon lost sight of Kay in the crowds that were pressing towards the tournament field.

A short while later, Arthur met Kay and Sir Ector coming the other way. Kay looked nervous and Sir Ector's face was grim.

"Follow behind us, boy," muttered Sir Ector, "and don't say a word."

They rode together in silence and the silence didn't stop until they reached the cathedral churchyard. They tied their horses at the gate and Sir Ector led the way to the marble block and the anvil.

In front of the block, Sir Ector turned to Kay. "Is this where you got the sword?" he asked.

"Yes, Father." Kay spoke quietly and his lips were trembling.

"Kay," said Sir Ector, "when you became a knight it was the proudest day of my life. Don't make me ashamed of you now. Do you swear on your honour as a true knight that you drew the sword out of the anvil and the stone?"

Kay's eyes flicked from side to side. "No, Father," he admitted.

"Then where the devil did you get it?" bellowed Sir Ector.

"Arthur brought it to me."

"Arthur?" frowned Sir Ector. "What do you mean, Arthur brought it to you?"

"It's true, Father – I mean, Sir Ector!" said Arthur. "You see, Kay left his sword at the inn, so I said –"

"Never mind Kay's sword, boy! I want to know about this one!" shouted Sir Ector, shaking the sword with the jewelled hilt. "Where did you get it?"

"From the anvil," said Arthur. "I was passing the churchyard and I saw the sword. Kay needed it, so I got it for him. Did I do something wrong?"

Sir Ector offered the sword to Arthur. "Put it back," he said, and the quiet way he said it was somehow more frightening than a shout.

Arthur placed the point of the sword into the slit on top of the anvil and pushed it down as far as it would go.

"Try and take it out, Kay," said Sir Ector.

Kay pulled at the sword until the veins stood out on his temples, but he couldn't budge it.

Then Sir Ector tried. His face went red and his eyes bulged. At last he let go of the sword with a grunt of defeat.

"I might as well try to pull a stone out of the cathedral wall!" he said.

"But it's easy," said Arthur. "Look!"

This time the sword glided out as though the anvil had been carved out of black butter.

Sir Ector and Kay fell to their knees and bowed their heads.

"What's all this?" laughed Arthur. "Are you playing a joke on me?"

But when Sir Ector spoke, there was no joke in his voice. "You don't know what you've done, do you? Didn't you read the words in the marble?"

Arthur turned and looked. Now he saw how strange it all was: the churchyard, the bright steel of the sword, the dark iron of the anvil, the glistening marble and the golden letters that glowed:

Whoever draws this sword from the anvil and the stone
is the true-born High King of Britain.

"Father, what does all this mean?" gasped Arthur.

"I'm not your father, Arthur," said Sir Ector. "You were brought to me when you were a new-born baby. I was told to raise you as my own son."

"Who told you?" said Arthur. "Who brought me to you?"

"The same man who made the sword, anvil and stone," said Sir Ector. "Merlin the Enchanter."

"Merlin?" Arthur repeated. "Who is Merlin?"

"I am," said a voice. The figure of a man stepped out of the shadows, or rather the shadows seemed to gather together to make him. He was tall and wore black robes that flapped around him like wings. "I am Merlin, and you are Arthur, the true-born high king."

"But I don't want to be high king!" Arthur burst out. "I just want to be a knight like Kay."

And suddenly he longed to hear the master-at-arms call him a lad again, because he didn't feel grown up at all.

Chapter Six
Uther's Son

ERLIN SPENT A LONG TIME TALKING to Arthur that morning in the churchyard. When the talking was finished, Arthur was more confused than when it had begun. He wasn't Sir Ector's son, Merlin said, he was the son of King Uther, the last High King of Britain.

"And my mother?" asked Arthur.

"The Lady Igraine," said Merlin. "After Uther was killed in battle, she died of grief."

A lonely feeling swirled inside Arthur. "So!" he said. "I came to London with a father and a brother and now I don't have anyone."

"The Lady Igraine had a daughter by her first husband," said Merlin.

"Then I've got a sister!" Arthur exclaimed.

"A half-sister," said Merlin. "Her name is Morganna."

There was a worried look on Merlin's face, but Arthur was too excited to notice. "When can I meet her?" he said. "Do we look alike? Do you think she'll like me?"

Merlin put his hands on Arthur's shoulders and smiled sadly. "You are high king," he said. "Don't try too hard to be liked. Kings can't trust anyone."

"Not even you?"

Merlin didn't answer, but he laughed silently with his eyes and teeth, like a dog-fox.

Arthur found it hard to believe what Merlin had said. So did all the knights when Merlin called them together on the tournament field and told them the news. He made Arthur stand on the back of a hay-cart so that he could be seen. Many of the knights were shocked.

"Why, he's only a boy!" one of them shouted. "How can a boy stop the wars?"

"He drew the sword from the anvil and the stone!" Merlin said.

"He should be playing with toys, not swords and crowns!" called out another knight. There was a lot of laughter at this. It reminded Arthur of the way Kay laughed at him and it made him angry. The anger gave him courage.

"Older people than I have tried to rule the country – and look at the mess it's in!" he cried. The knights fell silent.

"I don't know if I can bring peace, but I'm willing to try," Arthur went on. "I'll need your help to stop the fighting, but maybe helping me will be a way of helping each other and the country and ..." Arthur shook his head. "Oh, I can't explain what I mean!"

The knights blinked and the spell was broken, but some of them were impressed by the way Arthur had held them in silence and made them listen.

"There's something about that lad," said one. "I couldn't have stood up in front of this crowd and spoken the way he just did."

"He's still just a boy!" said another.

"What does it matter?" said a third. "We need peace."

"You're winning them! Speak again!" Merlin urged Arthur.

"But I don't know what to say!" Arthur whispered.

"Look at me!" said Merlin.

Arthur looked down into Merlin's face. Merlin's black pupils began to spin like wheels, and with each turn a year passed. In his mind, Arthur saw himself, older. He saw a circle of faces and armour glinting in firelight.

"There'll be a round table," he said, raising his face to the crowd, "big enough for a hundred knights to sit at. They'll be the bravest and the best in the world. They'll help me to keep the peace once it's won – by fighting if they have to. If there's evil, or cruelty, then the knights will ride out and put a stop to it. And they won't do it to get money, or power. Being a Knight of the Round Table will be something money and land can't buy. It'll be more important than that!"

Some knights cheered his words, others laughed scornfully.

"Was that all right?" Arthur asked Merlin. "Did I make them see it?"

"The best of them will understand," said Merlin.

Arthur didn't know what Merlin meant, but who did? The Enchanter's thoughts ran deeper than his words, and his magic ran deeper still.

Chapter Seven
THE CHALLENGE OF LORD PELLINORE

RTHUR WAS CROWNED IN WALES IN the ruins of the Roman fort at Caerleon – the Castle of the Lion. Merlin, Sir Ector and Kay were there, together with all the knights who had seen something special in the lad on the back of the hay-cart.

Others didn't come. The crown had hardly been placed on Arthur's head before a messenger arrived with a letter from a knight called Lord Pellinore. He sent Arthur a toy knight on horseback and said that he hoped Arthur's nursemaid would let him play with it.

When Sir Ector read the letter he was furious. "Raise an army, Lord King!" he said. "Pellinore will soon change his mind when he sees our battle flags!"

"Father's right!" Kay agreed. "Your enemies are all waiting to see what you do about Pellinore. If you let him get away with this insult, they'll think they can do just as they like."

Arthur felt all the knights staring at him, waiting for him to tell them what to do. "Will I have to make war to bring peace, Merlin?" Arthur asked. "It doesn't make sense."

"You must do what you think is right," Merlin replied. "It must be your choice, not mine."

"Then we must fight," Arthur told his knights. "If I don't rule the whole country, then being king means nothing. But we must fight fairly! Anyone who surrenders and swears loyalty to me will get a full pardon."

"That's no way to make war!" protested a hot-headed knight. "All your enemies must die, Lord King."

"That's the old way of doing things!"

The voice was so powerful that everyone turned to see who had spoken. It was Sir Gawain. "We must do as King Arthur says," said Gawain. "We can't unite the country with blood."

He looked at Arthur and smiled, and though it didn't seem the right time for smiling, Arthur smiled back. He suddenly felt that he'd found a friend, and he'd never had a friend before.

In the times that followed, Arthur came to realise that he needed friends badly. The noblemen who refused to have him as their king visited King Lucius of France and asked for help. Lucius gave them money and men. He knew that if Britain went on weakening itself with civil war, it would be easier for him to invade.

Time after time, powerful nobles marched out with their armies to fight the boy-king. Time after time, Arthur defeated them in battle, though not all the fighting was as fair as Arthur had hoped. War turned out to be dirty, uncomfortable and often boring. The new king made mistakes, though fewer than many people had expected, and he fought with such courage that many of his enemies were turned into loyal supporters. Sir Ector told Arthur that he was a brilliant leader but Arthur didn't think so.

He just tried his best to use his common sense in the mess and muddle of battle.

Of all Arthur's enemies, none gave him more trouble than Lord Pellinore himself. When Arthur captured his castle, Pellinore refused to surrender. He escaped to Scotland, raised a rebel army and marched against the king. He was defeated in a bloody battle, but once more he escaped, and this time he seemed to vanish completely. Pellinore was annoying, but Arthur couldn't help admiring his bravery and strength of will.

After a long search Pellinore was found in Wales. He was living alone in a rocky valley where three streams met and fell into a roaring chasm. Across the chasm stretched a narrow bridge. Pellinore waited in full armour on his side of the bridge, waving his sword and shouting curses at anyone who came near. Several knights who were anxious to please the new king challenged Pellinore to single combat. He beat them all.

"Go back to your boy-king and tell him to come himself next time!" he roared after them as they limped away.

And Arthur did come, on a bright summer morning. When Pellinore saw the company of knights Arthur had brought with him, he laughed and began sharpening his sword against a stone.

"Come on then, lads!" he called to the knights. "I'll take you on one at a time, and when I've finished with you I'll cross this bridge and snap your boy-king over my knee."

"Lord Pellinore," said Arthur, "swear loyalty to me and I'll give you back your castle and your lands. I need brave men like you."

"Aye, to do your fighting for you because you have no courage of your own!" sneered Pellinore. "Why don't you cross over and fight me face to face?"

Arthur swung himself off his horse and walked towards the bridge. Kay dismounted and ran after him to block his way, Gawain following close behind.

"Are you mad?" said Kay. "Pellinore will carve you up."

"I have to fight him, Kay," said Arthur.

"You're acting like a fool!" snapped Kay.

"Sir Kay," said Gawain sharply, "you forget that you're talking to the high king. Step aside."

Once more, Arthur and Gawain smiled at one another, and then Arthur set off across the bridge.

"He's just showing off!" Kay hissed angrily. "He wants to prove to everybody how brave he is."

"He wants to prove it to himself," Gawain said wisely.

Above the roar of the falling water, Arthur seemed to hear the voice of his master-at-arms. "Take your time, lad! Hold your shield high!"

Arthur wished he could remember all the other things the master-at-arms had told him, but when the fighting started he was too busy to remember anything.

They fought until their armour was dented and they were both cut and bleeding. They fought until the rims of their shields were ragged. Morning became noon and it was so hot that the air shivered, but still they fought on, their swords clanging and sparking as they came together.

Then Pellinore threw down his shield, raised his sword in both hands and brought it crashing down with such strength that it shattered the blade of Arthur's sword and knocked the young king on to his knees.

Pellinore raised his visor and wiped blood and sweat from his eyes. "Do you surrender, boy?" he asked hoarsely.

"No!" said Arthur defiantly.

"Surrender or I'll hack you in two!" Pellinore growled.

Arthur looked at the stump of his sword. It was the one he had drawn from the anvil and the stone. The dream of being high king now seemed as broken as the steel in his hand.

"I'll never surrender, to you or anyone!" he cried.

He flung himself at Sir Pellinore, wrapping his arms around his waist and pulling. Pellinore was taken by surprise and toppled over. Something struck the side of Arthur's head and a bright light flashed in front of his eyes.

Behind the light was a darkness that swallowed him down.

Chapter Eight
A SECOND SWORD

IF HE WAS DEAD, THEN DEATH WAS nothing like as bad as he had expected, Arthur thought. It was so peaceful – no shouting, no fighting and no decisions to make.

But slowly the blackness turned into Merlin's eyes and robes and Arthur found himself lying under a blanket on a soft bed of bracken. A fire crackled nearby and on the other side of the fire stood Merlin, gazing down at him.

"Where am I?" asked Arthur.

"Somewhere safe," Merlin replied.

Arthur tried to sit up, but it made his head hurt so much that he fell back with a cry. "You're lucky not to have lost your brains," Merlin told him. "Single combat with Lord Pellinore, indeed! How could you be so foolish!"

"I'd forgotten about the fight," said Arthur. "What happened?"

"Pellinore kicked you as he fell," said Merlin, pouring liquid from a leather bottle into a small cup. "When he got up, he laid his sword at your feet and swore loyalty to you. He said you were so brave he would rather fight by your side than against you. He called you Pendragon – dragon's head – because of your courage. Donkey's head would be more like it." Merlin handed the cup to Arthur. "Drink this in one swallow."

It tasted so sour that Arthur's eyes watered, but the pain in his head vanished almost at once. "Did I just drink magic?" he said.

"No, medicine," said Merlin, "but it's time for magic. Your sword was broken. Britain cannot have a king without a sword. You must get another."

The Enchanter pointed to the sky. Arthur looked up and saw the full moon. "Come with me," Merlin said.

They walked between trees until they came to the shore of a lake. Moonlight made the water shine white. A boat appeared, bearing three maidens who wore robes as white as the moon. The boat came to rest where Merlin and Arthur stood. Merlin stepped in and told Arthur to follow. Once he was on board, the boat glided towards the centre of the lake. It had no sails or oars and didn't rock like other boats Arthur had been in. He knew that it was moved by magic and the hairs on the back of his neck prickled.

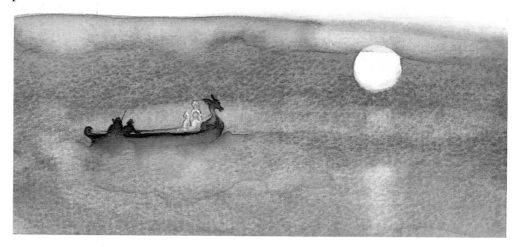

No one spoke until the boat came to a standstill, then Merlin said, "Look!"

Something was happening to the light on the water around them. It grew brighter, and as it brightened Arthur saw a sword the colour of moonlight rise out of the lake beside the boat. The sword was held by a hand that came straight up out of the shining water. "Take it," said Merlin.

Arthur's heart punched against his ribs. He reached out with shaking fingers. As soon as he gripped the hilt, the hand in the water slid under the surface without a ripple.

It felt as though he were holding moonlight and magic in his hand. "Is it really mine?" he whispered.

"The sword's name is Excalibur," said Merlin. "For a time it will be yours, though there will come a day when you will have to give it back. Until then, its power is joined with yours."

By the time the boat returned to the lake shore, Arthur could hardly keep his eyes open. He stumbled towards the distant camp fire gleaming between the trees.

"When you wake, it will seem as though you dreamed all this," Merlin said, "but Excalibur will be by your side."

"Yes," mumbled Arthur.

He didn't understand what had happened, or what was happening. All he understood was sleep. And when he reached his bracken bed he almost collapsed on to it.

"Nothing is ever finished," he heard Merlin say. "Remember, just when you think things have come to an end, they will be only beginning."

"Of course," Arthur murmured. "Anything you say, Merlin ..."

And then sleep took him.

Chapter Nine
Sir Leo's Daughter

NO ONE CALLED ARTHUR 'BOY-KING' again. When he drew Excalibur it seemed that nothing could stop him and he won victory after victory. Over the next two years he grew up fast and worry made him look older than he really was.

One evening in late spring, he was resting in his tent after battle when Merlin appeared before him, silent as a shadow.

"What is it this time, Merlin?" he asked wearily. "Another rebel lord? Another castle to capture?"

"The war is over," said Merlin. "The last rebel lord has been defeated and you are High King of Britain. You have fought your last battle for a long time."

Arthur sighed with relief. "So it's finished at last!" he said.

"Nothing is ever finished," Merlin reminded him. "The war has ended, but peace has begun. You must always be on your guard against King Lucius of France … and you must build yourself a castle. The High King of Britain must have a home."

"Can't I rest for a while and do nothing?" Arthur grumbled. "What's the point of winning if I never have time to enjoy it?"

"You're like the flame of that candle on your table," said Merlin. "You hold back the darkness, but you must burn yourself out doing it. Tomorrow you are going on a journey. Choose a companion to go with you and send the other knights home."

"Home!" Arthur said. "Two years ago, my home was Sir Ector's castle. Now I don't have one."

"You do, but you must search for it," said Merlin. "When you find it, raise your castle there. Look for an old place where new things can begin. Travel west."

When Arthur looked up from the candle, Merlin had gone.

Next morning, Arthur said goodbye to his army. The knights had fought long and hard together, and though they were glad to be returning to their families, they were sad at parting.

Arthur took Gawain with him on his journey. Kay was offended at not being chosen and sulked, until Arthur told him that he was going to be one of the Knights of the Round Table.

As Arthur and Gawain rode together, Arthur chatted happily at first, and then more seriously. "Can you forget that I'm your king and let me talk to you as a friend?" he said.

"I'll try," said Gawain.

"I've been thinking about what will happen after my castle is built and I've chosen the Knights of the Round Table," Arthur said. "What shall I do then? I know about being a king in wartime, but I don't know where to start with peace!"

"Do what other people do," Gawain said. "Get married and raise a family."

"But I don't know anything about marriage, or love," said Arthur. "How will I know when I want to marry someone?"

"You'll just know it," shrugged Gawain.

"That's a great help!" Arthur snorted. "That's like one of Merlin's answers – more confusing than the question!"

They stopped at many beautiful places, but they were all too marshy or too rocky to build a castle on.

On the seventh night, he and Gawain camped on top of a hill. It was too dark to see where they were exactly and they simply rolled themselves in blankets and fell asleep on the ground.

The sun was high when Arthur woke. He found that he and Gawain had been sleeping inside the grassy walls of a hillfort that had been built long before the Romans came. Leaving Gawain to sleep, Arthur walked to the top of one of the walls. The countryside stretched out in front of him. He could see fields and villages and, on the plain below the hill, a small castle. From its single tower, long banners waved lazily in the breeze.

He looked down at his feet, saw the fresh grass and the summer flowers and knew that this was the place Merlin had spoken about – an old place where new things could begin.

"Where is this?" he wondered aloud.

"Camelot," said a voice, "and you've got no right to be here! It belongs to my father."

Arthur turned and saw that a young woman had been watching him from the shelter of a blossoming thorn tree. She was half hidden in its branches and white flowers circled her black hair. Her eyes were dark brown and they flashed angrily.

"I'm sorry!" said Arthur. "I didn't know. My friend and I – "

"Well, you know now!" the young woman said. "Camelot Hill belongs to Sir Leo, and I'm Sir Leo's daughter. I like to come up here to look at the view and I like to do it alone!"

"Oh," said Arthur. "You see, the thing is – "

"What I see is a great, clumsy fellow trespassing on my father's land!" the young woman snapped.

Arthur knew that he should always be polite to ladies, but he began to laugh. He couldn't help it. Here he was, High King of Britain and Sir Leo's daughter was treating him like a ragged beggar.

Something about Arthur's laugh and the way his eyes sparkled made the young woman want to laugh too, but she stopped herself and frowned instead. "Are you laughing at me?" she said.

"Yes!" gurgled Arthur. "I mean – no, of course not!"

His mistake only made things worse. He hadn't laughed for two years and now that he had started, he didn't know how to stop. He fell on to his back and kicked his legs in the air.

When the laughing was over, Arthur felt wonderful. He sat up and grinned at the young woman. She blushed at his stare, but she didn't look away. She was beginning to feel curious about the young stranger who wore such a fine sword.

"What's your name?" she asked.

"Arthur. What's yours?"

"Guinevere," said the young woman, forgetting her pride for a moment. Then she remembered it. "It's not polite to ask a lady her name. You should wait to be introduced by –." Guinevere stopped. Her eyes grew round and startled-looking. "You're not Arthur the king, are you?" she whispered.

"Yes," said Arthur, "but it's all right. I mean, I don't mind that you got angry and told me off. Hey! Where are you going?"

Guinevere was so ashamed that she ran to where her horse was tied, jumped into the saddle and galloped off towards her father's castle. Arthur watched her ride away.

Gawain came up to him, yawning and rubbing his eyes. "I heard voices. Who were you talking to?" he asked.

"Lady Guinevere, Sir Leo's daughter," Arthur told him.

"I've heard of her," said Gawain. "People say she's quite pretty."

"Quite pretty?" Arthur exclaimed. "She's the most beautiful lady I've ever seen!" He hadn't meant to say it and he didn't know that it was true until it was said.

Gawain burst out laughing. "If only you could see the look on your face!" he said.

Arthur didn't have the faintest idea what his friend was talking about.

Chapter Ten
MERLIN'S GIFT

HEN SIR LEO HEARD THAT ARTHUR wanted to build his castle at Camelot, he was delighted. He wouldn't even let Arthur pay him for the land.

Arthur didn't know very much about building castles, and he soon found out that he knew even less than he thought. He had to speak to stone masons and carpenters who used words that he didn't understand, but he nodded as though he did.

It would take months before the building was finished and Arthur had to live somewhere in the meantime, so he accepted Sir Leo's invitation to stay in his castle. This meant spending a lot of time with Guinevere, and Arthur noticed how the hours sped by when he was with her.

What with castle-building and making a list of names for the Knights of the Round Table, Arthur wasn't aware of the passing months until, suddenly, it was Christmas. The hall of Sir Leo's castle was hung with branches of holly and pine and there was a lot of feasting and dancing. Arthur was too clumsy to be a good dancer, but Guinevere was wonderful – at least, so Arthur thought. When she danced he couldn't look at anyone but her, and every night he saw her dancing in his dreams.

Late one afternoon, Arthur was alone in the library. He was pretending to be working on the list of knights, but he was really thinking about Guinevere. She was so much in his thoughts that when he looked up and saw her standing before him, for a moment he couldn't tell if she was real.

"You look serious, Lord King!" Guinevere said.

"Don't call me that," said Arthur. "It makes me think that you're talking to my crown, not me. Sometimes I wish I wasn't a king, then things might be easier."

"What things?" asked Guinevere.

"I've been happy here with you and your father," Arthur said. "When Camelot is finished, there won't be time for us to go riding, or share jokes together. I won't be able to see you as often. That makes me sad."

"It makes me sad too," said Guinevere.

Arthur made a face. "Why should being king make me sad all the time?" he grumbled.

"You're not sad, you're just feeling sorry for yourself," said Guinevere.

"It isn't fair!" Arthur cried. "If I want to be with you and you want to be with me, then – "

"Yes?" said Guinevere.

"Then we should get married!" Arthur said in a rush.

It was dusk now. Guinevere's eyes were still shining in the shadows.

"Could we?" he said. "I mean, do you want to be queen?"

"No," said Guinevere, "but I want to be your wife."

"You mean, yes?" said Arthur.

"Yes," said Guinevere.

Arthur was so excited that he jumped up out of his chair. "Oh, er – should I kiss you now, or something?" he said.

"I think that would be a good idea," Guinevere smiled.

Next morning, Arthur and Guinevere rode up to Camelot. The castle was almost finished and they walked in the great hall together, their voices echoing up in the rafters above their heads.

"Where will the Round Table be?" asked Guinevere.

Arthur stood in the centre of the hall and held out his arms. "Here!" he said. "We'll sit round the table as equals, face to face, and make decisions together."

As he spoke, something happened to the light and the shadows at the far end of the hall, and Merlin was there. He looked thinner and more tired than the last time Arthur had seen him.

"Great things will be done here," said Merlin. "Sad things too. And because of them, the name of Camelot will last for ever!"

He raised his hand and light came out of it. The light twisted and curled and became a dragon, whose red-gold wings stretched from wall to wall. The dragon circled, slowly at first, then faster and faster until it touched the tip of its nose against the tip of its tail to form a ring of red light. The ring sank to the floor and vanished.

A round table stood where the light had been. A red dragon had been painted in its centre, and spreading out from the dragon like the spokes of a wheel were lines that divided the table up into a hundred equal parts. There were some names written around the edge of the table in golden letters:

King Arthur, Queen Guinevere, Sir Gawain, Sir Kay ...

"All the names on my list are here!" Arthur cried.

"Other knights will come," said Merlin. "When they take their places, their names will appear on the table with the others. This is my wedding gift to you, my last gift. My time in your story is over and my magic and I must rest."

Merlin turned away from Arthur and Guinevere and walked back towards the shadows. "Great things and sad things," he repeated. "Remember!"

And he was gone, leaving Arthur and Guinevere alone in the great hall of Camelot with the Round Table between them.

Chapter Eleven
Morganna's Smile

ARTHUR AND GUINEVERE WERE MARRIED at Camelot in the spring. Hundreds of people came to the wedding and the celebrations lasted for a week. The couple were given many presents, but the best one of all, for Arthur, came on the third day.

As he stood in the great hall with Guinevere to greet the guests arriving for the evening banquet, a young woman entered. The hall fell silent and everyone turned to look at her. She had a beautiful face with smooth skin, and fair hair that hung over her shoulders. As she walked towards Arthur and Guinevere, the only sound that could be heard was the hem of her dress brushing the floor. The young woman curtsied and held out a small wooden box. "My wedding gift to the king," she said.

When Arthur opened the box, he found a ring inside. The ring was made of a reddish-coloured gold and was shaped like a dragon biting its own tail. "It's beautiful!" he said.

"It once belonged to King Uther," said the young woman.

Arthur's hand trembled so much that he almost dropped the ring. "Where did you get it?" he asked quietly.

"King Uther gave it to my mother, and my mother gave it to me," the young woman explained. "My mother was the Lady Igraine..." The young woman lifted her head and looked straight at Arthur. Her eyes were dark and old, like Merlin's eyes. "My name is Morganna," she said.

"M-Morganna?" stuttered Arthur. "Then I'm your brother – and you're my sister – and – " He couldn't think what else to say, so he helped Morganna to stand up and then gave her a hug.

The silence was broken as everybody in the great hall started talking at once. Arthur insisted that Morganna sat next to him and he talked to her so much that his food went cold.

At last, Guinevere managed to get his attention. "You're ignoring the other guests. It's bad manners," she said.

"But I've got lots more questions I want to ask!" said Arthur.

"Then they must wait for another time," said Guinevere.

"Tomorrow!" Arthur told Morganna. "You are staying the night, aren't you? Stay for a few days! You can come and live here, if you like – there's plenty of room!"

When the meal was over, the dancing began, led by Arthur and Guinevere.

"Morganna is amazing!" Arthur said. "When she talks about my mother and father, it's as though I can see them standing in front of me! It's like magic!"

In another part of the hall, Kay sat alone, staring at Arthur and Guinevere as they danced. Kay had drunk so much wine that he hardly noticed Morganna when she sat in the chair next to his.

"Aren't you Sir Kay, the King's foster brother?" she asked.

"That's right," said Kay, without taking his eyes off Arthur and Guinevere. "He used to be my squire – now look at him! He's got it all: the crown of Britain, a beautiful wife, a fine castle ..."

"You sound jealous," said Morganna.

Kay turned angrily. He was going to tell Morganna to mind her own business, but before he could speak, she smiled at him. It was such a wonderful smile that Kay's anger vanished.

"Why should I be jealous of Arthur when I'm talking to the most beautiful lady in Camelot?" he said.

Morganna did spend the night in the castle, but she didn't sleep. Long after everyone else had gone to bed, she stayed by the window in her bedroom. Her shutters were open and moonlight shone on the water in a bowl she held. Morganna lifted the bowl and breathed on the water. First it went misty, but when the mist cleared Morganna could see a picture of Kay. He was asleep on top of his bed, fully dressed.

"You fool!" whispered Morganna. "In the morning you'll think about me – and before long you won't be able to think about anything else!"

She smiled as she spoke. It was an evil smile and Kay would have shuddered if he had been able to see it.

Chapter Twelve
LANCELOT

HEN THE WEDDING FEAST WAS OVER, knights came to Camelot. Some had been invited to be Knights of the Round Table, others were hoping to be invited. Among them was Sir Lancelot of the Lake, and when Arthur heard that Lancelot was at Camelot he was amazed.

Although born in Britain, Lancelot had grown up in France and had become a knight there. He was the greatest knight in France. Some said that he was the greatest knight in the world.

"He thinks too much of himself, if you ask me," said Kay.

"I think he's shy," said Gawain. "No one wants to talk to him because they're frightened of offending him and getting into a fight."

"I don't understand why he wants to be a Knight of the Round Table," said Arthur.

"King Lucius of France must have sent him to spy on us!" Kay said angrily. "Send him away!"

"I've got a better idea," Gawain said to Arthur. "If you want to know why he's here, why don't you ask him?"

Lancelot was surprised when King Arthur sent for him early next morning. When he entered the great hall, he had another surprise, because Arthur was alone and dressed in ordinary clothes instead of a crown and royal robes.

Lancelot went down on one knee. "Majesty –" he began and then he stopped, because Arthur burst out laughing.

"Oh, do stand up!" Arthur said. "You look silly. I want to talk to your face, not the top of your head."

"I'm sorry, sire," mumbled Lancelot, rising to his feet. "In the court of King Lucius, everyone had to –"

"Do you like riding, Lancelot?" Arthur interrupted.

"Of course, Majesty!" said Lancelot.

"Let's go for a ride, then," said Arthur. "And don't call me majesty. Don't call me Sire, or Highness, or anything like that. I can't get to know you with those fancy names getting in the way."

They rode down Camelot Hill, then followed the river north towards a thick wood. It was misty and the air was cool.

"Why did you leave France and come here?" Arthur asked.

"Because I was sick of it!" said Lancelot. "Lucius used to be a good king, but now he's greedy for money and power. He listens only to people who flatter him and he's started to believe what they say." Lancelot looked straight at Arthur. "I want to serve an honest king, someone who's better than I am."

They were in the wood now. There was quiet for a while, because Arthur was thinking of what to say.

"I try to be honest, but it isn't always easy," he said at last. "I don't know if I'm better than anyone else, but I want to be a good king and put things right. Being a Knight of the Round Table isn't about serving me really. It's about working together to –."

Something moved on the road ahead. First it was just the mist, then there was the sound of hoofs and a knight on horseback came galloping along the road. He was dressed in black armour. The helmet was shut to hide his face and he was pointing a lance at Arthur.

Arthur was so surprised that he couldn't move. The figure charging at him through the mist seemed like something out of a dream.

Lancelot had no weapons – not even a shield – but he didn't hesitate. He rode straight at the Black Knight, leapt out of his saddle and knocked him on to the ground.

The clatter of the armour hitting the earth made Arthur jump. His right hand reached down to draw Excalibur, but then he remembered he had left the sword at the castle. Arthur rode towards the struggling figures, though he had no idea what he would do when he reached them.

The Black Knight stood up and drew his sword. Lancelot lay dazed at his feet, unable to move away. Arthur saw the Black Knight raise his sword. "No!" he shouted. "Stop in the name of the king!" He had wanted his voice to boom like thunder, but it came out more like a screech.

The Black Knight half-twisted and tried to slash at Arthur as he passed. As soon as his head was turned, Lancelot sprang up, wrapped his arms round the Black Knight's neck and tried to pull him off balance. Instead, Lancelot pulled off the stranger's head – or so it seemed. The headless armour dropped to its knees, and then fell to pieces. There was no body inside it.

Arthur got off his horse and came running over. "What happened, Lancelot?" he said. "We can't have been attacked by an empty suit of armour! It isn't possible!"

Lancelot reached inside the black helmet and brought out what looked like a piece of twisted wood.

"What's that?" asked Arthur.

"The root of a mandrake plant," said Lancelot. "And can you smell something strange?"

Arthur sniffed, then coughed. "What is it?" he gasped.

"I've smelled it once before," said Lancelot. "It's the smell of witchcraft."

Chapter Thirteen
MORGANNA'S TAPESTRY

SIR ECTOR WAS WAITING AT THE GATE when Arthur and Lancelot returned. "Something's happened!" he said. "Come and see!"

They followed him into the great hall. All the knights were there, talking among themselves. Arthur saw at once what they were talking about. Lancelot's name had appeared on the Round Table, between Guinevere's name and Kay's. The golden letters glowed as though they were hot.

"It wasn't there last night!" said Kay. "What does it mean?"

"It means that Merlin's magic is still working and that Lancelot has been chosen as one of us," said Arthur. "Kay, bring me Excalibur and I will make Lancelot a Knight of the Round Table."

Arthur didn't notice the scowl on Kay's face as he turned away. On the way back to the great hall, however, Kay met Morganna, and she noticed his sour look at once.

"Has Arthur made you his squire now?" she said.

"Lancelot is going to join the Round Table," Kay said sulkily. "Some of us fought at Arthur's side for years to earn our places!"

"Did you fight at Arthur's side, or in his shadow?" Morganna asked. She leaned closer to Kay and spoke softly. "Come to my room and see me later," she said. "There's something I want to show you." She walked off without waiting for Kay's reply. She knew he would come.

Kay carried Excalibur to Arthur. Arthur drew the sword from its scabbard. Lancelot knelt and Arthur touched him on each shoulder with the flat of the blade.

"Rise, Sir Lancelot, Knight of the Round Table," Arthur said.

It should have been a time for celebration, but when all the

knights had taken their seats at the table, Arthur told them what had happened in Camelot Wood. The air seemed to turn cold.

"Witchcraft?" said Gawain. "Are you sure?"

"I'm certain," said Lancelot.

"But who would use witchcraft to harm the king?" asked Sir Ector.

"Someone who hates him," said Lancelot. "We must all be on the lookout for a traitor."

After the meeting was over, Arthur went to find Guinevere. He told her about the Black Knight and what Lancelot had said. "It was a horrible moment!" Arthur said. "You could see everybody looking round, wondering if one of us had done it!"

"But how can that be?" said Guinevere. "None of your knights practises black magic!"

"Who knows?" said Arthur. "Witchcraft is a secret thing. Oh, I wish Merlin was still here! He'd know what to do!"

While Arthur and Guinevere talked, in another part of the castle Morganna was showing Kay a tapestry that she was sewing. The bright colours of the silk threads shone in the shadowy room. Kay could see Camelot, the river and the wood that lay to the north. On the left of the tapestry was the figure of a knight.

"That's me, isn't it?" laughed Kay.

"Of course," smiled Morganna, filling a cup with wine. "I've sewn you into my tapestry and captured you. By the time I've finished, all the Knights of the Round Table will be there."

She handed Kay the cup of wine. He drank it without taking his eyes off the tapestry and then he held out the cup for more.

"Tell me," Morganna said quietly, "what happened in the great

hall this morning? What did Arthur talk about?"

Kay seemed not to hear her. "Where are you going to put Lancelot on your tapestry?" he said.

Morganna could already hear the whine in Kay's voice.

"Yes, let's talk about Lancelot," she said. "Tell me everything you know about him."

That evening at supper there was a terrible scene. Kay was drunk and staggered to his place, bumping into people and knocking things over. Many heads turned to stare at him.

"What are you all looking at?" Kay snapped. "You've seen me before, haven't you? I'm Kay, the King's foster brother! I'm the one who fetches his sword, just like he used to fetch mine!"

"Kay!" Sir Ector said sternly. "I think you should go to bed before you make a fool of yourself."

"I'll tell you who's making fools of us all with this talk of witchcraft," Kay said. "Lancelot! King Lucius of France sent him here to make trouble! He's trying to make us suspect each other. There was no witchcraft in Camelot until Lancelot came!"

Everything went quiet. All eyes were fixed on Lancelot. "Sir Kay," Lancelot said quietly, "if you weren't a Knight of the Round Table, I would challenge you to single combat for what you have said. Why don't you follow Sir Ector's advice and go to bed?"

Kay's face looked like a mask. His skin was white and there were blue half-circles under his eyes. "You don't frighten me, Lancelot!" he hissed.

Arthur sprang to his feet. His chair clattered to the floor behind him. "I didn't make you Knights of the Round Table for this!" he said. "We're supposed to fight evil, not each other!"

"Lancelot is evil!" Kay cried. "He's a traitor and a warlock!"

Lancelot stood and bowed politely to Arthur. "My lord," he said, "this quarrel was none of my making, but Sir Kay has gone too far." He turned to Kay. "We will settle this in the courtyard at sunrise tomorrow," he said.

As Lancelot walked out of the hall, many turned their heads to watch him go – but not Arthur. He stared at Kay and tried to understand why he was being such a fool.

Chapter Fourteen
A Witch in Camelot

ARTHUR WENT TO SEE KAY THE NEXT morning while it was still dark. He was surprised to find Morganna in Kay's room.

"I came to give Sir Kay this," she explained, holding up a green silk scarf. "If he ties it round his left arm, it will bring him luck."

"He doesn't need luck, he needs some sense!" Arthur told her. "Kay, why don't you tell Lancelot you're sorry before it's too late? I'm sure that if you both talk things over –"

"There's no point in talking to Lancelot," said Kay. "I meant what I said last night and if you weren't so wrapped up in all your grand ideas, you'd see that I'm right!"

"Why are you being so stubborn?" asked Arthur.

"You've never known what I was like!" snapped Kay. "This is my fight, Arthur, so let me get on with it and stop trying to interfere!" He left the room, pushing his way past Arthur to reach the door. Arthur felt sad as he watched him go.

"I've spent my whole life saying the wrong thing to Kay," he told Morganna. "Everything I do seems to offend him."

"You are the king," said Morganna. "If he doesn't obey you, you should throw him in the dungeons!"

"But I don't want to be that sort of king," Arthur said.

At sunrise, knights began to gather in the courtyard. Among them were Sir Ector and Gawain. Sir Ector looked worried.

"I don't know what's got into Kay recently!" he said. "He's always been a bit quick-tempered, but now he's drinking too much and it's not good for him. He sneers at everything. He just hasn't been himself since Lancelot arrived."

"Don't you mean, since Lady Morganna arrived?" said Gawain.

"Lady Morganna?" frowned Sir Ector. "What's she got to do with it?"

"Perhaps more than anyone thinks," said Gawain.

At that moment a fanfare of trumpets sounded and the king and queen arrived with the rest of the knights.

"What were you saying about Lady Morganna?" Sir Ector asked, but there was no answer. Gawain had gone, and Sir Ector couldn't see him anywhere.

Lancelot and Kay entered the courtyard and stood on opposite sides. They were dressed in full armour. Lancelot spoke first.

"Sir Kay! Last night you called me a traitor and a warlock. Will you take those insults back?"

"I will not," said Kay.

"Then you must fight," said Lancelot, and he drew his sword.

It was a fierce fight. Kay was the stronger, but Lancelot was quick. When Kay swung his sword, Lancelot ducked and spun round like a dancer. Kay seemed clumsy next to him. Their swords rang when they came together, followed by the dull clank of sword on shield. The sounds echoed round the castle walls.

Morganna was watching from her window, high up. In one hand she held her tapestry and in the other a needle.

"Poor fool!" she whispered, as she stuck the needle into the side of Kay's picture.

Down in the courtyard, Lancelot thrust his sword under Kay's left arm. The point of the sword slid between two plates of armour and Kay cried out in pain. He dropped his sword and fell to his knees, clutching his side.

"Sir Lancelot, I surrender to you!" he gasped. "You're no traitor, or warlock, but a true knight!"

Kay just managed to finish speaking before he fell in a faint.

Up in her room, Morganna laughed – and then the laugh stopped in her throat as she realised she was no longer alone. Someone had crept into the room without her hearing and was staring at her. It was Gawain.

When Kay came round, he found himself in bed. He saw Arthur in a chair on the other side of the room.

Arthur got up when Kay opened his eyes. "The doctor says you'll soon be better, but it's a deep wound and you must rest," he said. Then his voice cracked, "Lancelot might have killed you, Kay! How could you be such an idiot?"

It was difficult for Kay to talk. His mouth felt dry. "It was Morganna," he said weakly. "She said things about Lancelot being a warlock. When she said them, I believed her. When Morganna says things, truth and lies get mixed up..." Kay winced at the pain in his side. "Send her away, Arthur! She's no good!"

"But she's my sister!" Arthur said. "This is like a bad dream!"

"No dream," said a voice.

Arthur turned and saw Gawain and Morganna standing in the doorway. Morganna's face was hidden in her hair.

"Here's your witch!" said Gawain. "I knew there was something wrong about her as soon as I saw her. This morning I left the fight and went to find her. She put a spell on Kay. That's how he was wounded."

"Morganna?" said Arthur. "Is it true?"

Morganna raised her head. "Yes, it's true," she said. "I became a witch to hurt you, Arthur, but Merlin has put a strong magic on you so my spells can't harm you. If I can't hurt you, then I'll hurt the people you love, like Kay."

"But ...why?" asked Arthur.

"Your father killed my father!" hissed Morganna. "Then when you were born, my mother died! You took her away from me, Arthur. When I was a child, I had no one to love! All I had was you to hate – and I won't stop hating until you and all your knights lie bleeding in the mud!"

Arthur couldn't bear to hear any more. He stepped forward to catch hold of Morganna and shake her into silence, but as he reached out, she faded and vanished. All that was left of her was the dead, rotten smell of witchcraft and the memory of her words.

"I'll hurt the people you love...I'll hurt the people you love..."

Her voice went round and round in Arthur's head, making him feel sick with fear.

Chapter Fifteen
THE WHITE STAG

OR A LONG TIME, WHAT ARTHUR HAD dreamed of seemed to come true. Whenever there was trouble or unfairness, a Knight of the Round Table would be sent out to put things right. The knights had many adventures and the fame of the Round Table spread to other countries.

When King Lucius of France heard about King Arthur and his knights, he burned with jealousy. More than once he tried to quarrel with Arthur and many people were afraid that there would be a war between France and Britain.

Besides the problem of Lucius, there was another matter that worried Arthur: he and Guinevere had no children. At first they had thought that children would come in time, but as the years slipped by they began to wonder if something might be wrong.

One evening, late in autumn, Arthur and Guinevere went to the top of a tower in Camelot to watch the sunset. It was a fine one, with a red sky and purple-gold clouds. Arthur was in a quiet mood and Guinevere asked him what was wrong.

"Time," he said. "It goes so quickly. I noticed some grey hairs when I looked in the mirror this morning. I'm getting old. Do you mind?"

"You've been growing older ever since we met," said Guinevere. "I'm used to it by now." Arthur smiled, but Guinevere could tell that he still had something on his mind.

"I wonder if Morganna put a spell on us so we can't have children," said Arthur.

"Perhaps," said Guinevere.

"If we did have children, which one of us do you think they'd look like? Would they have dark hair, like yours?" asked Arthur.

"You'll make us both unhappy if you go on talking like that," said Guinevere. "If we've been cursed by Morganna, then it's our unhappiness that she wants. We mustn't let her have it!" She rested her head on Arthur's shoulder. "You're not the only one who's growing old. Sir Ector's hair is white and Kay's got many more grey hairs than you!"

"Lancelot doesn't look any older, though," said Arthur.

A cold breeze made Guinevere shiver. "Let's go inside."

"Guinevere," said Arthur, "do you ever wish –"

"Never," Guinevere interrupted. "I'm too busy being happy to make wishes." Though they didn't know it, it was one of the last happy times for Arthur and Guinevere. The sadness that Merlin had talked of was getting closer every day.

It began on a morning when there was a frost. Guinevere loved frosty weather and she loved riding. Arthur was too busy to go with her that morning, so he sent Kay to keep her company and to be her guard. Kay brought with him a new knight, Sir Mordred. Mordred was a young man and he was full of new ideas about fighting. Kay enjoyed arguing with him.

"Gunpowder will change everything," Mordred said as they rode along. "Cannon will blow walls into dust. There won't be any long sieges in the future – battles will be fought in minutes instead of hours."

"Nonsense!" said Kay.

"Just think," said Mordred, getting carried away. "If King Arthur had a cannon, he could kill hundreds of enemies at once. King Lucius wouldn't dare go to war with him!"

"Being a knight isn't just about killing people, Mordred," said Kay. "It's about being noble and fair. What's noble about blowing up people with gunpowder?"

Guinevere clicked her tongue and her horse trotted ahead. She felt the cold wind running through her hair and it made her laugh. She clicked her tongue again to make the horse gallop into Camelot Wood. It was too fine a morning to be talking about war and killing.

The wood was gloomy and filled with winter shadows and Guinevere was startled when something bright flashed on to the track in front of her. But her alarm quickly turned to wonder. It was a stag, but no ordinary stag. It had red ears, silver antlers and its coat was as white as frost. The creature was so beautiful that when it ran off the main path Guinevere followed, riding deeper and deeper into the heart of the wood.

Guinevere felt compelled to follow the stag. She knew the feeling was strange and that she ought to be frightened by it, but she couldn't help herself. She wasn't even frightened when she saw a castle, even though she knew there was no castle in Camelot Wood. The castle glowed pure white and the stag ran in through its open gateway with Guinevere close behind.

As soon as she was inside the courtyard, the castle gates slammed shut. Guinevere's horse reared in fright and threw her. Her head struck the ground and all the shadows of the wood seemed to come down in front of her eyes.

It was some time before Kay and Mordred arrived, shouting Guinevere's name. They had tracked her into the middle of the wood, but they found no white castle there. All they found was a white stone, as tall as a man on a horse. They saw hoof prints leading up to the stone, but the ground all around was unmarked.

Mordred jumped down from his horse and stamped the earth to make sure that it was solid. "The queen can't have disappeared into the stone, can she?" he cried.

Kay felt the worst fear he had ever known in his life. "Back to Camelot!" he said hoarsely. "We must tell the king at once."

Chapter Sixteen

In the White Castle

CAMELOT WAS IN CHAOS WHEN KAY AND Mordred arrived. The courtyard was crowded with knights being helped into armour by their squires. Grooms were saddling horses. Blacksmiths were sharpening swords on grindstones that sent out showers of sparks. Kay stopped a passing squire and asked him what was happening.

"Haven't you heard the news, sir?" the squire said excitedly. "King Lucius of France has landed with an army at Dover. They're marching on London."

Arthur was with Lancelot, Sir Ector and Gawain in the great hall. They were looking at a map that had been rolled out on the Round Table. When Arthur heard that Guinevere was missing, he turned pale. "I must find her!" he gasped.

He made as though to leave, but Sir Ector stopped him.

"My lord," Sir Ector said, "the queen may need you but the kingdom needs you more. You must lead your knights into battle against Lucius."

Arthur knew that Sir Ector was right. He felt miserable and helpless.

"I'll go to Camelot Wood and search for the queen," said Lancelot.

"Let Mordred and me go with him," said Kay. "It's our fault that the queen is lost."

So King Arthur rode out of Camelot at the head of his knights with Gawain at his right hand and Sir Ector at his left. Sir Ector carried the banner of Britain: a blood-red dragon on a white background. The armour of the knights flashed like silver in the wintry light as they turned on to the road that led to London.

Lancelot, Kay and Mordred rode the other way. Mordred was in a bad temper. "I wanted to go into battle with the others!" he complained to Kay. "They're going to get all the glory!"

"Battles aren't glorious, they're horrible," said Kay. "I ought to know, I've fought in enough of them."

"Yes!" Mordred said bitterly. "When you were young you had lots of chances to go into battle and become famous! Well, I'm young and I want my turn!"

By now the sun was high in the sky, but inside Camelot Wood it was as gloomy as dusk. No birds sang and the drumming of the horses' hoofs on the ground sounded hollow. This time, Kay and Mordred did see the white castle and, as they drew near, it grew so cold their breath smoked on the air. "This wasn't here before!" cried Mordred. "What magic is this?"

They got down from their horses and walked towards the closed gates. High up on the wall above the gates was a bell, and as they watched a rope slithered down from it like a snake. On the bell was written:

If you are a brave, true knight, then ring and enter.

Before Lancelot or Mordred could stop him, Kay ran forward and pulled the rope. The bell made a hard, iron sound. The gates swung silently back, just enough for Kay to step inside, and then they closed behind him.

Lancelot and Mordred waited. No sound came from within the castle. Every second the air seemed to get colder and the shadows deeper.

"Why is Kay taking so long?" Mordred said at last. "I'm going in to find him."

"You'll stay where you are," said Lancelot. "I'll go. If I'm not back by sunset, take the horses and return to Camelot. Don't stay in this place after dark."

Lancelot stepped up to the rope and tugged it. Once more the bell rang and once more the gates swung open. Lancelot drew his sword and entered.

After the gates had shut, Mordred stood staring at them for a while, then he paced about, slapping himself to try and get warm. The cold made his temper even worse.

"They left me here to mind the horses as if I was a child!" he grumbled to himself. "But I'll show them! I'll be one of the most famous Knights of the Round Table one day!"

"Yes, you will ..." said a voice.

Mordred drew his sword and turned in one movement. The voice had come from behind him, but all he could see was shadows and trees and the cold, white castle.

"Who's there?" he asked.

"You'll be one of the most famous knights who ever lived," the voice promised. "Kings will fall down in front of you ..."

There were more words, but Mordred stopped listening to

them. All he could hear was the voice. It stroked him like a gentle hand and made him feel warm. He felt so comfortable that when someone stepped out of the shadows and trees and walked towards him, he didn't feel afraid. It was a young woman, dressed in dark green. She had fair hair and when she smiled at Mordred he saw that she was beautiful. His sword fell from his hand.

"That's right, Mordred," said the young woman. "You must listen carefully and do just as I say."

Mordred didn't want to do anything except stare and stare at her. "Who are you?" he whispered.

The young woman laughed. She threw back her head and her hair rippled. "Names don't matter, Mordred," she said. "All that matters is my eyes. Look into my eyes and listen to my voice …"

Chapter Seventeen

THE SLEEPERS IN THE SNOW

HEN LANCELOT ENTERED THE GATES OF the white castle, the cold took his breath away. All around, frost glinted on white stone and icicles like glass fangs hung from the roof.

Kay was stretched out on his back in the middle of the courtyard. Lancelot hurried across to him and almost tripped over his sword. It lay on the ground, its blade thick with ice. Kay's eyes were closed and his skin looked blue.

"Kay?" said Lancelot. "Can you hear me?"

He knelt and touched Kay on the shoulder. Kay's armour was so cold that Lancelot could feel it through his glove.

A sound made Lancelot look up. A knight dressed in white armour and carrying a huge battleaxe was striding towards him. A deep voice boomed out of the White Knight's closed helmet. "I am the guardian of Castle Winter! Why have you come here!"

"I seek Guinevere, the queen," said Lancelot, rising to his feet.

"That lady lies asleep in this castle," said the guardian. "She will not wake again until the day comes when I am beaten in single combat."

"That day has come," said Lancelot.

The guardian laughed long and loud. "What is your name, boastful knight?" he asked.

"Sir Lancelot of the Lake, Knight of the Round Table," Lancelot said.

"Well, Sir Lancelot," said the guardian, "after I have killed you, I will nail your helmet to the gates as a warning to others!"

So saying, the White Knight swung his axe. As it came through the air, it made a sound like a moaning wind. Lancelot dodged to one side and struck out with his sword. Its point screeched against the White Knight's armour. Once more the axe blade flashed down, and this time Lancelot did not move quickly enough. The edge of the axe caught his left shoulder. A cold, aching pain stabbed down his left arm, making his fingers numb.

"You feel the pain in your arm, Sir Lancelot?" said the guardian. "Before long it will spread to your heart and freeze it solid!"

Lancelot fought on with his left arm dangling uselessly by his side. He could feel the cold pain moving from his shoulder into his chest. The White Knight was forcing him back towards a corner. Once he was trapped there, Lancelot knew he would be done for. He tried to jump to his right, then his left, but each time the axe's moaning blade stopped him.

Then Lancelot gathered all that was left of his strength, lifted his sword as high as he could and brought it down. The sword split the White Knight's helmet down the middle. The guardian of the Castle Winter roared and his voice became a roaring wind. Snowflakes blew into Lancelot's eyes and stung his face.

The blizzard was fierce but short. It blew itself out as quickly as it had begun and when it was over the White Knight and the white castle were gone. In their place was snow, as deep as midwinter. Lancelot saw Kay to his left, still lying on his back, but no longer blue. He was snoring loudly. A little way in front of Lancelot, Guinevere lay asleep, her black hair spread out on the snow. Lancelot tried to walk to her but stumbled and fell.

"I must rest!" he whispered.
"Just for a little while …"

As soon as Lancelot fell asleep, Morganna appeared. Mordred was beside her, his eyes glowing with a greenish light. They walked towards Lancelot and Guinevere, but only Mordred's feet left prints in the snow.

Morganna crouched beside Lancelot and reached into a pouch at her belt.

"Is he dead?" asked Mordred.

"No," said Morganna. "They will all live. When you wake them their wounds will be healed and Guinevere will remember nothing about how my magic held her prisoner."

"Why bother to wake them?" grinned Mordred. "Why not let me stab them while they sleep?"

"I have another plan," said Morganna. "One that will cause Arthur to suffer for a long time." She took a small bottle out of the pouch, poured a drop of liquid on to her finger and touched Lancelot's lips. Then she did the same to Guinevere.

"Is it poison?" said Mordred.

"It's a love-potion," said Morganna. "When they wake and look at one another, Lancelot and Guinevere will fall in love at once. Their love will grow with each passing day until it tears the Round Table apart!"

Chapter Eighteen
THE WORKING OF THE POTION

AY WOKE UP AND SAW MORDRED leaning over him. Mordred's face looked so strange that Kay didn't recognise him at first.

"Are you all right, Mordred?" he said at last.

"Yes, I'm all right. But what happened to you?" Mordred replied.

"I went in through the gate of the white castle and then ..." Kay shook his head. "I don't remember the rest. Where's Lancelot?"

"He's over there, talking to Queen Guinevere," said Mordred. "They're both safe."

But Lancelot and Guinevere were not safe. Morganna's evil love-potion was working on them. Lancelot gazed at Guinevere and she returned his gaze. Their hearts were so full that they could hardly speak, but words came at last. "I thought I knew what love was," said Guinevere. "I thought I loved Arthur, but now I see he's more like a dear friend than a husband."

"And I can see only you, and how there will never be a time for our love," said Lancelot. "I must leave."

"Where will you go?" asked Guinevere.

"Away from Camelot," Lancelot replied. "If we don't meet again for a long time, perhaps we can forget our feelings."

"I'll never forget," said Guinevere.

"Neither shall I," said Lancelot, and he turned away to join Kay and Mordred.

Hardly a word was spoken on the ride out of the wood. Lancelot and Guinevere were too afraid to talk and Kay was deep in thought, trying to remember what had happened in the Castle Winter. Mordred rode behind the others, smiling to himself.

When they rejoined the main road, Lancelot reined his horse to a stop. "I'm going to find the king and tell him that the queen is safe," he said.

"What, now?" said Kay. "Rest and eat first!"

"The sooner the King knows, the sooner his mind will be at ease," said Lancelot.

But Guinevere knew it was because of her that Lancelot was leaving. As she watched him ride off, a tear rolled down her cheek. She brushed it away so quickly that Kay didn't notice she was crying, but Mordred did and his smile grew wider.

Lancelot rode east. The sun set and evening came, but Lancelot didn't stop. When night fell he rested his horse and while it drank from a stream he stared at the sky. The stars made him think of the light in Guinevere's eyes and the blackness of the night was like the colour of her hair. He couldn't stop thinking of her. He threw himself into the stream, hoping that the icy water would help him to forget, but it was no use. He stayed awake and shivering all night, and when dawn came he set out again.

It was late in the afternoon when Lancelot found Arthur and the knights. Arthur, Gawain and Sir Ector were in a clump of trees on top of a ridge. They were watching the French army, which was making camp in the valley below.

Arthur was overjoyed when he heard about Guinevere, but when his relief wore off he looked at Lancelot and frowned. "You look tired out," he said.

Lancelot's hair was uncombed, his cheeks were prickly with stubble and streaked with mud and his eyes stared wildly. "I'm all right," said Lancelot. "When do we attack?"

"Not until morning," said Gawain. "A few of us are going to ride over to the other side of the valley when it gets dark. At sunrise, we'll attack the camp and pretend to run away. When the French follow us, the rest of our knights will charge down the ridge and take them by surprise."

"Let me lead the raid at sunrise!" said Lancelot.

"You don't look as if you could lead a horse into a stable!" Gawain said.

"I'll be all right when I have slept," Lancelot insisted.

But Lancelot didn't sleep and when morning came his eyes were wilder than ever.

The battle went as Gawain had planned. Lancelot and the raiding party attacked the French camp and then rode off with arrows whistling around their ears.

"To your horses!" Lucius shouted to his men. "See how the Knights of the Round Table run from us like frightened cats!"

Laughing scornfully, the French knights charged after the raiding party. They left the defences of their camp and formed a long, straggling line.

Then, at the mouth of the valley, Lancelot and his men turned, while scores of British knights poured down the hillsides. King Lucius realised that he had ordered his men into a trap.

Poems were written afterwards about the battle that was fought that day in the valley. The poets said that the air was so thick with arrows the sky went dark. They said that when the two armies clashed, the sound was louder than thunder. Many brave knights – British and French – died that day because of King Lucius's jealousy and pride. Many brave deeds were done, but nobody was braver than Lancelot. Wherever the fighting was fiercest, he was there. He threw away his helmet and shield and used both hands to hold his sword. His armour dripped red and he struck fear into the hearts of his enemies. Nothing could stop

him; even when an arrow went through his armour and into his right leg, just above the knee, he went on fighting.

At midday, Lucius surrendered. He knelt on the battlefield, handed over his sword and promised Arthur that he would never invade Britain again.

"I don't believe a word Lucius says," Arthur told Gawain afterwards.

"Don't worry," said Gawain. "As long as you've got fighters like Lancelot on your side, you've got nothing to fear from Lucius."

"Where is Lancelot?" asked Arthur. "I haven't seen him since the battle. I hope he's having that arrow-wound seen to."

But Lancelot wasn't with a doctor. In the confusion at the end of the battle, he had snapped off the shaft of the arrow in his leg, taken off his armour and ridden away. He didn't know where he was going, he only knew that he couldn't go back to Camelot and that the pain in his heart hurt more than the pain in his leg.

By the time darkness fell, Lancelot was burning with a fever. Sweat streamed down his face. He seemed to see the guardian of Castle Winter riding down the road towards him, lifting his great battleaxe. Lancelot raised his arm in front of his face, cried out in fear and tumbled from his horse.

For a long time, Lancelot lay senseless at the side of the road. He would have frozen to death if someone hadn't found him. A monk, riding back to his monastery on a little grey donkey, saw the wounded man lying by the road, stopped and went over to him. He saw that the man was still alive, but only just.

"Dear, dear!" the monk said to the donkey. "I can't help him while he's lying here, can I? We must carry him to the monastery. The abbot will know what to do!"

Chapter Nineteen
GUINEVERE'S TRIAL

HEN LANCELOT WENT MISSING, A GREAT sadness came over Camelot. Most people thought that he had been killed in the battle. A few hoped he had somehow lost his memory and was alive.

Guinevere was heartbroken, though she couldn't show it. She turned in on herself and became quiet. She didn't laugh any more and sometimes when Arthur spoke to her, it seemed that she didn't hear him. To try and forget about Lancelot, Guinevere filled her time with work. She visited the cottages of people who were poor and sick and made sure they had enough money to buy food and medicine. But nothing could take the thought of Lancelot from her mind, and in the end her good deeds were turned against her.

Without Lancelot, the glory of the Round Table faded. Many knights had been killed in the battle against Lucius, and they were replaced by young men. Their hero was Mordred. He taught them about gunpowder and cannon. They copied his ideas and they even copied the way he dressed, wearing black clothes and suits of armour that bristled with spikes.

Mordred was Morganna's eyes and ears in Camelot. Through him she was able to spread the poison of her evil. The Knights of the Round Table no longer spoke their minds face to face. They met in secret in dark corners, or whispered behind their hands. Mordred made sure that most of the whispering was about Guinevere.

Arthur knew nothing about the rumours, but he sensed that something was wrong in Camelot and he talked about it to Kay, Sir Ector and Gawain.

"It's these young knights!" said Sir Ector. "They talk back and snigger and show no respect for their elders!"

"The world is changing," said Kay. "I don't like the changes any more than you do, Father, but they can't be stopped!"

"It hasn't been the same since we lost Lancelot!" sighed Sir Ector. "He was the best of us!"

"Yes," agreed Arthur. "If only I could be sure of what happened to him."

"Why not send some young knights on a quest to find out?" suggested Gawain.

The more Arthur thought about Gawain's idea, the better it seemed. He called a meeting of the whole Round Table and when everyone was seated he talked about the quest for Lancelot.

"So," Arthur said, "who wants to set out on this quest?"

"Not I," said Mordred. "Sir Lancelot is dead, my lord. Treason killed him and the traitor is still here in Camelot."

"What do you mean?" cried Arthur.

Mordred pointed at Guinevere.

"The queen used magic to drive Sir Lancelot mad and his madness drove him to seek his own death in battle!"

Some knights jumped to their feet, shouting that Mordred was right. Others shouted in support of Guinevere and for a while there was chaos in the hall. Then Arthur drew Excalibur. The blade flashed like lightning and there was silence.

Arthur was angrier than anyone had ever seen him. His voice was choked with rage when he spoke. "Do you dare to accuse the queen of witchcraft?" he asked Mordred.

"I do, and I call her to answer my charge in front of the Round Table!" Mordred replied.

"Very well," said Arthur. "And when she has answered it, Mordred, you and I shall meet in a fight to the death!"

Guinevere had to stand and listen while Mordred accused her of dreadful things. He called poor villagers to speak against her, saying that after she visited people, they died. One woman said she'd seen Guinevere dressed in green, dancing in the moonlight holding a dead child above her head.

When Mordred had finished speaking, Arthur put Excalibur on the Round Table and told Guinevere to place her right hand on the hilt.

"I swear on this sword that I am not a witch," Guinevere said. "I never danced in the moonlight. If people died after I visited them, then I'm sorry – but it wasn't my fault."

Arthur breathed a sigh of relief and turned on Mordred. "As for you – " he began, but Mordred interrupted him.

"Let the queen also swear that she and Sir Lancelot were never in love! Let her swear that Lancelot wasn't mad with love for her when he last left Camelot!"

Guinevere's eyes grew wide. She opened her mouth as though to speak, then closed it again.

"Guinevere?" said Arthur. "Tell them it's not true!"

"I can't," said Guinevere, and though she spoke quietly her voice filled the hall.

"I say the queen is guilty of treason and witchcraft!" shouted Mordred. "She must be burned at the stake!"

Guinevere hardly heard what he said. All she noticed was the hurt in Arthur's eyes.

Chapter Twenty
THE INNOCENT QUEEN

GUINEVERE WAS PUT IN PRISON AND NEWS of her guilt was sent across the land.

Arthur felt numb. He shuffled about like an old man and spent hours alone, staring at the wall. When Gawain came to see him, Arthur spoke as though he was talking to himself. "It's all my fault," he mumbled. "I didn't know how to be a husband ..."

"You must do something," said Gawain. "This is all some plan of Mordred's. We must fight!"

"Fighting settles nothing," said Arthur. "All it does is cause problems that lead to more fighting."

"My lord," said Gawain, "you may lose the Round Table as well as the queen!"

"Great things and sad things!" sighed Arthur. "That's what Merlin said. Merlin knew everything ..."

A bonfire was built outside the castle and covered with canvas to keep it dry. A great crowd gathered around it, some sorrowful, some curious, some laughing cruelly, as though Morganna's evil had spread from Camelot into the whole country.

The morning of the execution was as black as night. Thunder rolled and lightning crackled across the sky. Rain lashed the faces of the crowd as the Knights of the Round Table came out of the castle in a solemn procession. A special platform had been built near the bonfire and they took their places on it.

Then Arthur came out, walking like a man half asleep. He climbed the steps on to the platform, sat heavily in a chair and covered his face with his hands.

Mordred was full of himself. He shouted orders to the men uncovering the bonfire and smiled and winked at his friends.

When Guinevere came out, the crowd were quiet. The queen walked between two guards with her hands bound, but she held her head up and did not look afraid. When the guards tied her to the post at the top of the bonfire, she did nothing to stop them.

At the foot of the bonfire the executioner waited with his flaming torch for Mordred's word. Mordred walked to the edge of the platform and looked out at the faces in the crowd. "The queen has been found guilty of witchcraft and treason!" he declared. "Executioner –"

"Stop!"

The voice was followed by a peal of thunder. A gap opened in the crowd. In the flash of a bolt of lightning, a monk appeared. He carried a long staff and his hood was pulled down over his face. His clothes were muddy, as though he had walked a long way.

"Let me pray with this woman!" he said.

"Keep back!" snarled Mordred. "Don't waste your prayers on a witch!"

The monk paid no attention to Mordred. Still holding his staff in his left hand, he clambered up beside Guinevere. Then he faced the crowd. "This woman is no witch!" he shouted.

The monk pulled back his hood. It was Lancelot. His hair was streaked with white and he had a thick grey beard, but there was no mistaking him.

"The queen has been under an evil spell!" said Lancelot. "The same spell bewitched me, but it was none of the queen's doing. She is innocent!"

There was terrible confusion. Some of the crowd cheered, some groaned and others scratched their heads, not knowing what to make of it all. No one noticed Mordred jump down from the platform. He seized the torch from the executioner's hands and thrust it into the bonfire. The wood had been soaked with oil and it caught light at once.

On top of the bonfire, Lancelot struggled with the ropes that bound Guinevere. By the time he had loosened them, he and Guinevere were surrounded by flames.

"Get behind me and put your arms around my neck!" said Lancelot. "Hang on as tightly as you can!"

He lifted Guinevere on to his back, and charged. They burst through the flames, landing on the platform in front of Arthur and his knights. Lancelot set Guinevere on her feet and bowed to the king.

"The queen is innocent," he said.

There was a shout behind Lancelot. He turned and saw Mordred rushing at Guinevere with his sword raised. Before he could strike, Lancelot's staff cracked down on his wrist and sent the sword flying. Mordred tried to draw his dagger, but Lancelot used the staff to send him sprawling.

Immediately, the knights who followed Mordred drew their swords and took a step towards Lancelot, but their steps faltered as Gawain appeared at Lancelot's side, closely followed by Kay, Sir Ector and twenty other knights.

Arthur's numbness left him. Suddenly everything seemed to make sense and he knew what he had to do. He stood up and walked over to Mordred, who had raised himself to his knees.

"Leave here, false knight!" said Arthur. "You're not fit to be a Knight of the Round Table!"

Mordred got to his feet and faced Arthur, his eyes burning green. "Your Round Table is too small for me, Arthur!" he said. "Your day is over. Britain needs a new king – King Mordred!"

He turned his back on Arthur and walked away. Many young knights went with him.

Chapter Twenty-one
THE LAST BATTLE

HAT NIGHT, LANCELOT TOLD HIS STORY, from the fight in Castle Winter to his return to Camelot. After his wounds had healed, he had decided to become a monk and forget his past.

"Gradually I began to realise that I was under a curse, and that my love for the queen had been caused by magic," he said.

"Morganna!" said Arthur.

"Yes," said Lancelot, "and you can be sure that she's the power behind Mordred. When I heard that the queen was to be burned at the stake, I left the monastery and came here because I knew that the time had come."

"What time?" asked Gawain.

"The fight with Mordred will be the last battle," said Lancelot. "When that is finished, nothing will be the same."

When all the others had gone to bed, Arthur and Guinevere stayed talking in the great hall. They stood together by the side of the Round Table. Guinevere noticed that the golden names were dull and peeling and the table suddenly looked old and worn.

"I'm going to the nuns at Almesbury," Guinevere said. "I hope to find the same peace in prayers that Lancelot found."

"I'm glad you will be safe," said Arthur. He looked hard at Guinevere, because he wanted to remember her face clearly. All sorts of things went through his mind and he knew he would never be able to say them all.

"If I had been Sir Arthur instead of a king, things would have been different for us, wouldn't they?" he said.

"Britain needed you to be king," said Guinevere.

Arthur took her by the hand. "When I'm...I mean, after the fight with Mordred is over, will you remember me sometimes?" he asked.

"Always," said Guinevere. Then Arthur raised her hand to his lips, and thus he and Guinevere parted for ever.

It seemed strange to be preparing for war in springtime. When Arthur and his knights rode out, the sun was bright and the fields were full of flowers. It reminded Arthur of his wedding, and the time when the war at the start of his reign had ended. His past and his present seemed to be coming together.

The last of the Knights of the Round Table made themselves ready for battle on the plain below Camelot Hill. They had the river at their back so they couldn't be attacked from behind. It wasn't long before Mordred and his army appeared.

There were thousands of them. Instead of silk banners, they carried animals' skulls on the tops of poles. Mordred's army formed a long, untidy line and shouted insults across the gap between themselves and Arthur's men. Mordred rode up and down the line. He wore a suit of dark-green armour with blades on the arms. On the crest of his helmet was a pair of horns. As he

rode past his men, they beat their swords against their shields and shouted his name until he held up his hands for silence.

"Knights of the Round Table!" Mordred cried. "Surrender to me now and take me as your king and I will spare your lives!"

Arthur's men stood firm. No one moved.

"Mordred," said Arthur, "put down your weapons while there's still time. Break the evil hold Morganna has over you! Come back to the Round Table!"

Sweat trickled down Mordred's face. His lips were grey. The side of his mouth twitched and he spoke in a harsh croak. "Never! We must fight to the death!"

It was a terrible battle. Men and horses screamed as Mordred's cannon blew them to bits and tore wide holes in the earth.

Smoke drifted across the battlefield in blinding waves, adding to the confusion.

Sir Ector died in the first charge of the battle. A cannonball exploded near him and he was killed instantly.

Kay died in the heat of noon, trying to reach Mordred. Mordred's bodyguards cut him down with axes, but not before Kay had killed two of them.

The fiercest fighters on the field were Arthur, Gawain and Lancelot. They stood shoulder to shoulder and their swords made a ring of death around them. Time and again Mordred's men charged and broke over them like waves breaking over a rock.

They fought until sunset, and then Arthur found he was swinging Excalibur at nothing. Lancelot lay in a faint, bleeding

from a dozen wounds, and Gawain stood over him, nursing a gash in his shoulder.

"Are we the only ones left?" asked Arthur.

"Not quite," Gawain said grimly. "Look behind you."

Arthur turned, and there was Mordred, holding a spear. His green armour was dented and streaked with blood. He had lost his helmet and his mad eyes glowed. "Surrender!" he shouted. "I am king! You must bow to me!"

Arthur shook his head wearily. "It's over, Mordred," he said. "Don't you see? Morganna never wanted you to be king. All she wanted was this!"

Arthur turned his head to the dead and the dying, and at that moment Mordred ran at him. Arthur felt the spear pass through his body at the same moment as the point of Excalibur found Mordred's heart and both men fell to the ground.

Chapter Twenty-two
THE RETURN OF EXCALIBUR

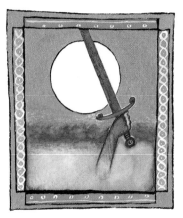

RTHUR LAY STILL FOR WHAT FELT LIKE a long time. He was in a black, peaceful place and he wanted to stay there, but there was something that he had to do first.

The blackness lightened to grey. He felt water in his mouth. He swallowed, coughed and opened his eyes. He saw Gawain, holding a helmet filled with water.

"Gawain!" said Arthur. "Excalibur ..."

"Is by your side," said Gawain. Tears shone in his eyes.

"There's no time to be sad," Arthur said. "Take Excalibur and throw it into the river."

"What?" said Gawain.

"It must be given back," said Arthur. "Do it, Gawain!"

Gawain went down to the river bank and stood there, staring at Excalibur. He thought of all the good that had come with it and how it could do no one any good at the bottom of the river. Gawain left the sword on the ground and returned to Arthur.

"Is it done?" Arthur asked.

"Yes," said Gawain.

"What did you see?" said Arthur.

"Nothing," said Gawain. "The sword splashed into the water, there were some ripples and that was all."

"You're lying to me, Gawain," Arthur said. "You've been my truest friend all these years, be true to me now. Throw Excalibur into the river. Watch carefully and tell me what you see."

Filled with shame, Gawain turned and went back to the place where he had left the sword. He didn't look at it as he picked it up. He swung it round once and let it fly out of his hand. Excalibur flashed in the light as it fell and then Gawain saw a hand rise up out of the river. It caught Excalibur by the handle, held it perfectly still for a moment and then slid back under the water, taking the sword with it.

When Arthur heard footsteps behind him, he thought it must be Gawain. "Have you done it this time?" he said.

"Don't worry," said Morganna's voice. "Your precious sword is safe now."

Arthur turned his head and saw Morganna staring down at Mordred's body. Her face was so beautiful and so evil that it was dazzling.

"Was this what you wanted?" Arthur asked her.

Morganna looked at him and smiled. "Yes," she said. "The Round Table is finished. You're lying in the mud with your dead knights and your smashed dreams, and I've won! I want you to think about that as you die!"

"No, Morganna!" Arthur said. "You've got what you wanted, but you haven't won. Your hate for me was the most important thing in your life. When I die, you'll have nothing."

Morganna saw that what Arthur said was true. She threw back her head and howled like a wolf at the red sunset. As her howl grew louder, she faded. Her dress turned from green to grey. The greyness spread into her face and hair and then suddenly she was there no more.

Arthur closed his eyes. He had meant to rest only for a few moments, but when he felt himself moving gently from side to side, he thought he must be fast asleep and dreaming. He opened his eyes and saw that he wasn't lying on the battlefield any more, but in a boat with three maidens who wore robes as white as moonlight. Standing in front of them was Merlin.

"I'm tired, Merlin," Arthur said. "Can I rest now?"

"Yes," said Merlin. "The time of knights and witches and enchanters is over. There's no place for us in the age that's

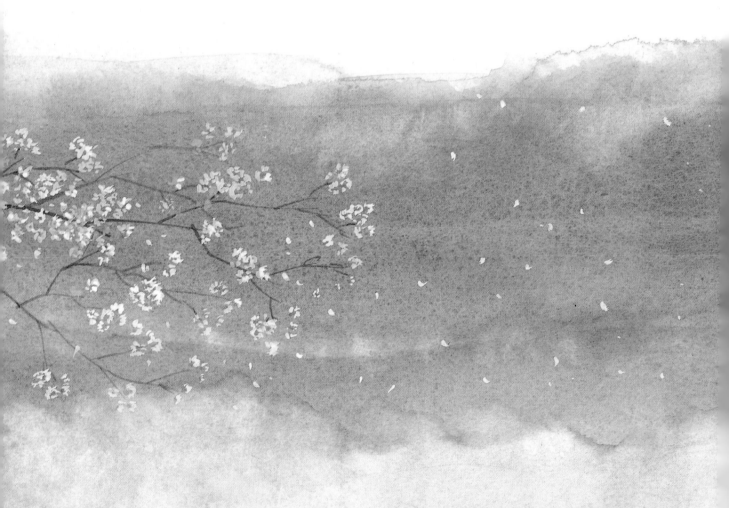

coming – not for a long while, at least. We can all rest now."

The banks of the river were lined with trees in blossom. As the boat glided under their branches, the trees showered down white petals. They reminded Arthur of the snow that had fallen many years ago, on the way to London with Sir Ector and Kay.

"It's a long journey," he murmured. "It's the longest journey I've ever taken."

The boat floated silently on as the sun went down over the horizon and the first stars began to twinkle in the evening sky.

AFTERWORD

SOME SAY THAT ARTHUR DIED THAT DAY and was buried at Glastonbury in Somerset. Over his grave was placed a stone, carved with these words:

Here lies the body of Arthur, who was once king of Britain and who will be king once again in the future.

Others say that Arthur didn't die at all, but went to join Merlin, who was asleep in a cave. There they wait, with the knights of the Round Table, waiting to wake and fight in one last battle, when Britain needs them most.